READING IS FUN!

IMAGINE THAT! ™

BOOK ONE

Written by
Ruth A. Radmore

Illustrated by
Isaak Lien

SPARKPRESS

Published by SparkPress, a BookSparks imprint,
A division of SparkPoint Studio, LLC
Tempe, Arizona, USA, 85281
www.gosparkpress.com

Published 2017
Print ISBN: 978-1-943006-38-0
E-ISBN: 978-1-943006-39-7

Library of Congress Control Number: 2017936150

Cover design by Isaak Lien and Tabitha Lahr
Illustrations by Issak Lien

Printed in Canada

INTRODUCTION

This book offers readers a chance to explore many different creative activities while developing their own imaginations. The story-poems offer experiences with artworks, construction, planning ahead, making decisions, and being aware of oneself. Although these unique stories were written for the elementary school levels, they offer enriching opportunities for those of all ages.

Every story is intended to increase the reader's interests and abilities. Small booklets of some of these same stories have been read and used by educators in Japan, Nigeria, France, Russia, and the United States. They were enjoyed by children in kindergarten and by student teachers at a European university. In each case, the stories received positive reviews by children, adults, teachers, administrators, and by those teaching and learning English as a second language.

The approach, stories, and information in this book offer far more than is available in any other children's book. It offers a wide range of ideas and creative activities to explore, experience, and enjoy.

— Ruth A. Radmore

ACKNOWLEDGMENTS

Rarely is any accomplishment achieved by one person. There are others who contribute in various ways. It is through their interest, encouragement, and support that a finished work is possible.

This book, *READING IS FUN! IMAGINE THAT!* has had the support of family and friends, through their words of enthusiasm and encouragement. Many have read and evaluated selections from the original booklets and have offered their valued responses and their interest in translating the stories for international publication.

It was due to the thoughtfulness of my husband, David, that the time and opportunity to write were available. His efforts were essential to my completing this first book and the rest of the series.

For children's books, words without illustrations are like songs without music. In this case, it takes the combination of words and visual images to invite readers into the stories and stimulate their own involvement in creativity.

If it were not for the extensive and capable abilities of the editor and project manager, Jan Kalish, this series would have remained as text in a computer and printouts in a file. Her responsibilities have encompassed ALL areas of the publishing process. She offered the professionalism and personal dedication that are paramount in achieving positive results. To Jan, and to all those who have made this initial undertaking possible, I express my genuine and lasting gratitude.

— Ruth A. Radmore

UNIQUE FEATURES OF THIS BOOK

These story-poems, activities, and information combine new concepts in children's books. They encourage reading, writing, artwork, and construction. The story-poems expand thought, imagination, creativity, and the reader's basic interests and abilities in various ways:

1. If there is an unfamiliar word, the reader simply turns two to three pages to find a list of words noted by page number. Each is defined and used in a sentence.

2. For those not accustomed to reading aloud, important words in each line which should be stressed are shown in larger, bold type.

3. Each story ends with a variety of activities which relate to the story. These give the readers the opportunity to use their own creative ideas through writing and artwork.

4. The entire book is ideal for use at school, home, summer camp, youth groups, and for learning English as a second language.

5. The imagination and creativity used in the story-poems and activities can encourage the reader to try other creative interests. Through these, it is possible to develop abilities that can be enjoyed for years.

6. Information about heredity and human growth provide valuable details for children to know. These topics are rarely taught at the primary school levels.

HAVE YOU EVER TRIED CREATIVE WRITING?

Writing can be a great adventure. A blank piece of paper is like an open invitation to put down your ideas about anything you see, think, or imagine. The possibilities are UNLIMITED. Once you try writing you may be surprised by your own excitement and ability. Those who are good at making up and telling stories may even decide to become authors. As you read the stories in this book, think about the ones that YOU would like to write. Then find paper and pencil quickly, before your surprising ideas slip away.

You could even stretch your imagination and write about people you have NEVER MET, and animals or creatures that DON'T EXIST. Your mind is an amazing place for discovering and exploring what interests you, and new things you want to do. The first step in anything is to give it a try and be surprised.

Some writers begin when they are very young and see things with a youthful point of view. Others start when they are older and have more time, experiences, and ideas to write about.

People have been writing ever since the first written language was used thousands of years ago. After all those years, there are still more writers and things to write about. You have your own thoughts and ideas that you could use and share. At EVERY age, people can find that **reading, writing, imagining, and creating are FUN**.

CONTENTS

WHY THESE 12 STORIES ARE SPECIAL

These story-poems help you in different ways. They make it easier to use your imagination, learn new words, and try new creative experiences. You'll have chances to write, do artwork, and much more, as you enjoy the **fun** of reading.

1. **Creative & Imaginative Thinking:** In the "What If" story, you will learn about a child who daydreams impossible things and enjoys his own imagination.

2. **Art Activities:** These stories invite you to try different art materials in ways you may not have tried before. Then you can make your own original designs.

3. **Planning Ahead:** There are many things that may happen in your future, and you may want to start thinking about them and planning for them now.

4. **Construction Activities:** Some of these materials you may not have used before. They can be used in many different ways. Imagination can help you make decisions about your own ideas when you create original constructions.

5. **Self-Awareness:** You'll learn a bit about yourself and things you do and why. You'll read about one child who was even able to find something good that came from things that had upset him.

6. **Decision Making:** There are often many choices to make, and these stories show ways in which people made wise decisions. You can even write or draw about choices you have made, or would like to make.

WHAT IF?
Creative and Imaginative Thinking

"**What If**" are like two **magic** words
that let your mind **create**.
They let you have **amazing** thoughts
that **you** originate.

It's really **fun** to picture things
that no one's **seen** before.
When you create your **own** ideas,
why not imagine **more**?

Your visions might be **fanciful**,
where **everything** you see
becomes a grand **adventure** that
you really wish **could** be.

What if you put on **wings** and **flew**
quite high above the **ground**,
and asked some birds to **fly** with you
so you'd have **friends** around.

You'd see the **mountains** as you passed,
some **woods** and **meadows**, too.
You'd watch as little **towns** appeared.
Oh, what a **lovely** view.

The folks below would be **amazed**,
surprised by what they **see**.
They'd smile and wave and call, "**Hello!**"
How **thoughtful** they would be.

Next, with **each step**, you'd stride a **mile** and find **lots** of places.
That way you'd meet folks **everywhere**, all with **kindly faces**.

3,700 miles

If you'd just touch an empty **plate** you'd make a **meal** appear.
Then you could fill a lot more plates for people **far** and **near**!

Then you could dig a "**problems**" hole
for **worries** that persist,
and once you'd **buried** all of them,
solutions could exist.

Next, what if you made brand new **socks**
that would be **heat** controlled,
so folks in **freezing** lands would find
they'd never feel the **cold**.

5

Today, why don't you touch the **sky**
and move the **clouds** about.
Perhaps you'll try to **squeeze** just **one**
and let some **rain** fall out.

What if the folks around the world
could feel like **family**?
They'd help each other solve their **needs**
and live more **happily**.

6

amazing things

what ifs

new thoughts

So many grand, **amazing** things
are stored in **every** mind.
If only I would "tease them **out**"
there might be **more** to find.

How many "**What Ifs**" have **you** saved
and kept them in your **head**?
I wish you'd **tell** a few of them
and share with **me** instead.

Our minds are full of **many** thoughts,
ideas completely **new**.
I'm sure you have a lot **yourself**.
Imagine That! You DO!

WORDS TO KNOW AND USE

After understanding each word, you can try making up a sentence that uses it. The numbers at the left refer to the pages where the words appeared. Some of the words in this story have other meanings too: See page 9.

2. **"magic"** is to have something seem impossible. "Jim can do magic tricks."
   "create" refers to making something new. "I create my own original artwork."
   "amazing" refers to something very unusual. "This sunset is really amazing."
   "originate" is doing something that no one has done before. It's your idea.
   "No one ever made anything like this before. How did you originate it?"
   "fanciful" is to be fancy and playful. "Your original story is very fanciful."
   "adventure" is an exciting experience. "Camping out was a new adventure."

3. **"appeared"** refers to being seen suddenly. "It just appeared out of nowhere."
   "surprised" is when something is unexpected. "You really surprised me."
   "thoughtful" is to do kind things. "It was thoughtful of you to help me."

4. **"everywhere"** means in every place. "It seems to be raining everywhere."

5. **"persist"** is to insist on doing things. "That child will persist in asking 'why.'"
   "solutions" refers to solving problems. "I've found some easy solutions."
   "heat controlled" is being able to keep an even temperature.
   "My room is comfortable because the furnace keeps the heat controlled."

6. **"squeeze"** is to press something. "I squeeze toothpaste from the tube."

7. **"tease them out"** is wanting something to happen, and helping it happen.
   "I tried to get my kitties from under the house. I finally teased them out."

ACTIVITIES

What unusual things can you think of that could make an imaginative story? Ideas can make impossible things seem real. New thoughts are interesting for others to read, and drawings can make them seem real. What unusual ideas do you have that would be fun to write about and draw for others to enjoy?

THINGS YOU HAVE JUST LEARNED

You've learned about a boy who used his imagination to do impossible things. No one else has your same thoughts, so your own are original. What amazing things can you imagine? By thinking, you can picture places that don't exist, and find things that are amazing. Your mind is growing and it's able to help you discover interests and abilities you didn't know you have. This requires thought.

Some words have more than one meaning. **<u>Floated</u>** may suggest either being in the air or on the water: "The swimmer floated when he was tired." **<u>Solutions</u>** can mean finding the right answers, but may also refer to liquids. "Kool-Aid is a solution of powder dissolved in water." **<u>Stride</u>** may be used to suggest improvement: "You've made a great stride in your reading ability." **<u>Stretch</u>** can mean that something can be made bigger or longer, or it can refer to a distance: "We still have a long stretch to go before we arrive home." Words are wonderful, and you need them to talk, write, and understand people. The more words you know, the more you can share your ideas, experiences, create stories, and tell of your hopes and dreams. By using words well, you **grow mentally**, and thoughtful words aid your **social growth**.

EARTH SCULPTURES
Art Activity

"Why are you playing in the **mud**?
That's what I **never** did,
except when I made **mud** pies once,
when I was just a **kid**."

"I think you haven't **noticed** that
these aren't just **pies** I've done.
I'm forming **sculptures** made with **earth**.
You might try **making** one.

"This dirt contains **adobe** soil,
adobe's like a **clay**.
It's dark, heavy, and holds its **shape**,
so forms will **stay** that way."

"When mud's wet **dirt**, without the **clay**,
   the shapes can fall **apart**.
Adobe is a **stronger** soil,
   and saves my work of **art**.

"Plain dirt when dry will crumble.
I'd lose what I have done,
   so I do everything I **can**,
   to try to save **each one**.

"I place a damp **rag** over it,
   to keep it **moist** and **strong**,
   then cover it with **plastic** so
   the sculpture's damp quite **long**."

"I wouldn't know quite how to **start**,
or what I'd like to **make**,
and since I've not **tried** this before,
I might make a **mistake**."

"Why don't you start by mixing **mud**,
to find out how it **feels**.
Just take your time, you'll be **surprised**
by things the mud **reveals**.

"There's one good thing, you can't **run out**,
since there's more **dirt** around.
If you don't **like** the thing you've made,
it goes back in the **ground**."

12

Clay
5+ years

Earth
1 day

"If mud were clay, we'd need a **kiln**.
Clay needs a **firing** phase.
The heat makes clay stay strong for **years**.
　　while mud just keeps for **days**.

"To have my work moved **easily**,
　I make it on a **board**.
Then when I'm **finished** for the day,
　I place it where it's **stored**.

"When I **began**, I couldn't think
　of anything to **make**.
So I just let the **mud** suggest
　directions I should take."

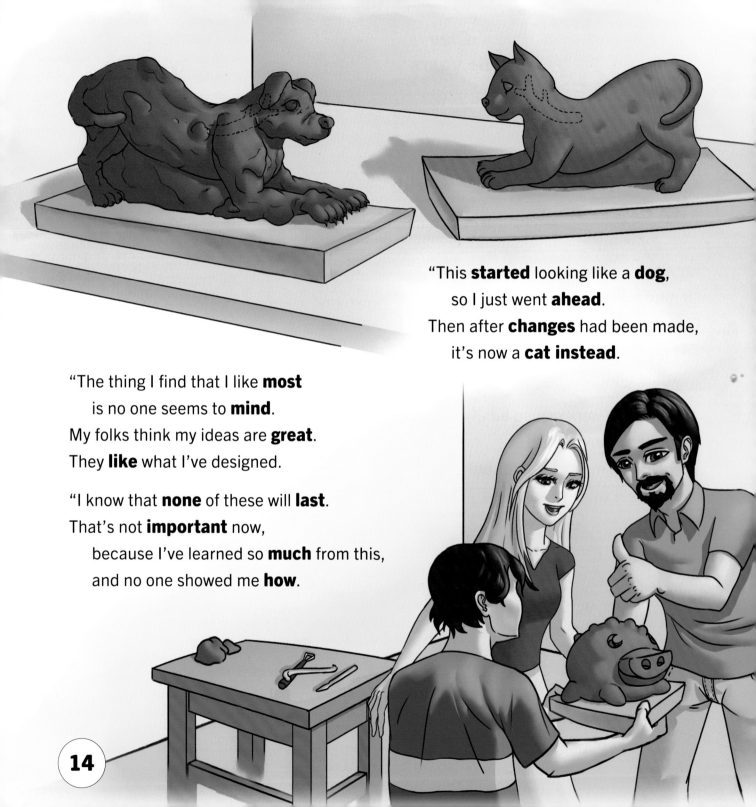

"This **started** looking like a **dog**,
so I just went **ahead**.
Then after **changes** had been made,
it's now a **cat instead**.

"The thing I find that I like **most**
is no one seems to **mind**.
My folks think my ideas are **great**.
They **like** what I've designed.

"I know that **none** of these will **last**.
That's not **important** now,
because I've learned so **much** from this,
and no one showed me **how**.

14

ELOY STEIN

"I've **saved** the **best** so I could take
a **few** of them to **school**.
My teacher made a nice **display**
that showed my **sculpture** tool.

"That's when some kids got **curious**,
and asked me how it's **done**.
I was surprised by their **response**,
when some tried **making** one.

"A **sign** was posted by my work,
then **others** tried it **too**.
A group of us are mud **sculptors**.
Imagine That! NOW YOU!"

ELOY STEIN

WORDS TO KNOW AND USE

After understanding each word, you can try making up a sentence that uses it. The numbers at the left refer to the pages where the words appeared. Some of the words in this story have other meanings too: See page 17.

10. **"except"** refers to something else that could be done instead.
> "I would have run home, except for the fact that I was too tired."

"forming" is to shape something or do something new.
> "We will be forming a cheering section for our school games."

11. **"damp"** refers to having water in it. "The rain made my coat damp."

12. **"surprised"** is how you feel when something unexpected happens.
> "I was very surprised to see them. They'd been away for a year."

"reveals" refers to something that appears or becomes clear.
> "When I use a telescope, it reveals things I have never seen."

13. **"kiln"** refers to a special oven used to make finished clay-work strong.
> "I put my clay bowl in the kiln to be fired."

"firing phase" is when the kiln is closed and the heat is turned on.
> "Later in the firing phase, the heat in the kiln was turned higher."

14. **"changes"** are things you do to make something different.
> "I've made some nice changes in my room, and I like it better."

"instead" refers to doing something different than you had planned.
> "Today I went to a friend's house instead of going home first."

"designed" refers to making something in your own special way.
> "I designed this Father's Day card by myself."

15. **"display"** refers to an exhibit. "The library has a new book display."

"curious" is wanting to know. "They were curious about the news."

"response" refers to an answer. "They waited for his response."

ACTIVITIES

Most people don't think of mud or sand as sculpture materials, but there are artists who use them. Even though it won't last long, there are HUGE sand sculpture exhibitions at some beaches. People go there to watch them being made. Why not try making your own sculpture using adobe mud? Then you could write a story about it and include a drawing of your sculpture.

THINGS YOU HAVE JUST LEARNED

Did you know there was sculpture material in your own garden or on vacant land? It's true that it won't last long, but it's fun to see what you can make. Once you start you may be surprised at how many ideas you have.

When you use new words, they are easier for you to remember. Someone might even ask you, "Where did you learn that word?" The more words you know, the more ideas you can talk about. Words help you to say exactly what you mean, so that you are more easily understood. As you get better at using new ones, you are growing mentally. If you are also using words to talk with people and share your ideas, this is social growth.

Be careful with words that have several meanings. **Crack** can refer to something that has been damaged. It can also be a comment that upsets people: "That crack you just made was not polite." It can also be used as a slang word meaning that something made you laugh: "You crack me up!"

PIGGY BANKS
Planning Ahead

I have **two** banks I keep at home,
  though neither bank has **locks**.
The larger one's a **plastic** pig,
  the other's just a **box**.

The plastic one's a **birthday** gift,
  the box I got from **Dad**.
I decorated it **myself**,
  with **art** supplies I had.

It's **hard** to take coins from the pig.
  I **shake** it till they **fall**.
The box can open faster since,
  I untie **strings**, that's **all**.

The money comes in **different** ways.
Gifts fill the **plastic** one.
The **box** holds cash that I have **earned**
for helpful **chores** I've done.

Whenever I discover coins
    just laying on the **ground**,
    I think they're something like a "**gift**,"
    although they're gifts I've **found**.

Those coins go in the **plastic** pig,
    they're mine to spend or **not**.
The money's used for **gifts** I give.
At times I'll buy a **lot**.

Some days I'll **spend** a dime or two
    if I have funds to **spare**,
    or buy a friend an **ice cream** bar.
I think it's nice to **share**.

I've learned that thrift is sensible.
I don't spend **carelessly**,
    or make a quick **decision** on
    some fancy **toy** I see.

I ask myself, "Will this thing **last**,
    or might it quickly **break**?"
If I lose **interest** far too soon,
    did I buy by **mistake**?

$100

$50

My folks have said they're **proud** of me
for **saving** tips I've learned,
like separating what I've found
from money that I've **earned**.

Someday I'll need a **downtown** bank,
and have my own **account**.
By then I'll work for **wages** and
might earn a **large** amount.

BANK

MENU

$1.99

$9.

21

For now, I'm really **happy** that
my banks aren't far **away**,
since I can count my "cash on **hand**"
so I keep **track** that way.

I'm sorry when someone has **lost**
the **coins** that I've found.
But I feel pleased with what I **earn**
from all my **chores** around.

22

Stock ranchers often raise some **pigs**,
   but I like **my** "pigs" **more**.
I feed them on my tasty **coins**,
   not **pig** food from a **store**.

My quiet "pigs" don't **bother** folks.
They don't grow **big** and **fat**.
I keep my "pigs" right in my **room**,
can you IMAGINE THAT?

23

WORDS TO KNOW AND USE

After understanding each word, you can try making up a sentence that uses it. The numbers at the left refer to the pages where the words appeared. Some of the words in this story have other meanings too: See page 25.

18. **"decorated"** is to make things attractive. "I decorated our Christmas tree."

19. **"chores"** are odd jobs around the home. "One of my chores is doing dishes."
    "discover" means to have found something. "A miner hoped to discover gold."

20. **"funds"** refers to money. "I plan to buy something special with these funds."
    "thrift" refers to spending money wisely.
       "Thrift is important to me, so I save for things I really want."
    "carelessly" means not being careful. "I used a dish carelessly and broke it."
    "decision" means to decide something. "My decision was to wait a while."

21. **"proud"** refers to a feeling of respect. "His big sister is so proud of him."
    "separating" means to put things in different places.
       "He was separating the two dogs so that they wouldn't fight."
    "account" refers to a bank's separate money records for people.
       "My parents helped me get my savings account at their bank."
    "wages" refers to money earned for working. "He earns good wages."

22. **"cash on hand"** refers to money that is kept close by.
       "I like to have a little cash on hand for small things I might need."
    "keep track" means to keep a record of where things are.
       "It's hard to keep track of our puppy. He likes to wander and meet folks."

23. **"stock"** refers to sheep, pigs, or cattle that are raised on farms or ranches.
       "There's going to be a special showing of stock at the fairgrounds today."
    "tasty" means to have a nice flavor. "That was a tasty lunch we had today."

ACTIVITIES

Do you have a special place to keep money that you find, earn, or are given? What things do you look forward to buying with money you have saved? Do you have odd jobs for which you are paid? What chores do you enjoy most, and what makes them more fun than other things you are asked to do? Have you ever thought about making your own piggy bank and decorating it yourself? Why not write a story about earning and saving money, and what you would like to save it for? You could even draw a picture of what you would like to buy.

THINGS YOU HAVE JUST LEARNED

Have you learned some new things about banks and finding, earning, and saving money? Did you know that when children are old enough, their parents may take them to a bank and open a savings accounts for them? This account can earn a little extra money each month. It's called "**interest**." "**Interest**" also refers to being curious about something. "He shows an **interest** in learning to play the guitar." A person might say, "That story is of **interest** to me."

Sometimes when you learn one word, you are really learning two. **Account** refers to a record of money, but it can be used to ask someone to explain something. "How do you **account** for the fact that you arrived home early?" **Stock** refers to farm animals, but also to things that are available to buy at a store. "This store has lots of **stock** on hand." This means that the store has many items for sale. There are many surprising things to learn about words and their meanings.

THE FIRST "GIFTS" WE RECEIVE

Long before we open our eyes for the first time, we have received special "gifts" from relatives we may never meet or hear about. These gifts are called "genes" and we inherit them through our parents and their close relatives. Someone may have told you, "You remind me of your mom," or "You have your grandfather's gift for music." These are inherited gifts.

A famous sculptor had been married four times and had a son by each marriage, yet the sons didn't meet until they were adults. At that gathering each shared his love for his special talents and work. One was a writer, another a choreographer who planned the movements to be used in a dance, the third composed music, and the fourth became an opera singer. Not one of them was a sculptor. Each had believed that his talents had nothing to do with anyone else. When his father had told one son that he was the one who had given him this creative gift, the young man simply said, "Aw Dad, don't take the credit for MY talent." It wasn't until this first meeting that the four sons talked together of their own creativities. Suddenly they all realized that these truly were treasured gifts from their father. The sons let him know how grateful they were for the creativity he had given them. Their talents had become a meaningful and valued part of their success and happiness.

Everyone receives special traits and qualities through their parents, but it is up to each person to develop those abilities and use them well. Are you aware of the special gifts you inherited from your mother and father?

WE GROW IN
FOUR DIFFERENT WAYS

From the time we are born, and through much of our lives, we continue to grow in four different ways:

Physically, our bodies grow: Bones, muscles, teeth, skin, hair, nails, as well as everything inside of our bodies. All of these continue to grow every day.

Socially, we can try to get along with family, friends, and others. We learn to be helpful, thoughtful, kind, fair, honest, and to develop many other social skills.

Emotionally, we become more careful about our feelings and reactions. We may naturally be happy or might easily become upset. It is possible for us to try to control our anger and other emotions that might cause others to be disturbed.

Mentally, our minds grow. We increase our abilities to think, reason, organize, make decisions, use our imaginations and creativity, and to follow directions.

We can help ourselves to grow in each of these four ways, simply by learning how and trying to improve. **Physically**, we can make an effort to be strong and healthy, and to avoid injury. **Socially**, we can try to be more considerate of the needs and feelings of others. **Emotionally**, we can try not to overreact. **Mentally**, we can improve our minds in ways we think, reason, plan, and learn.

As we grow, we change and mature. We can become the person we WANT to be, by the choices and decisions we make and by trying to improve.

THE MUSIC MAKERS

Construction Activity

Since instruments can cost a **lot**,
let's find **another** way.
We'll use some well-made makeshift ones
that some of us can **play**.

I talked with several **friends** of mine
and said to **make** or find
some different kinds of "**instruments**"
to play when they're **combined**.

We'd like to form an **orchestra**
and test the **sounds** we make.
No instrument can **cost** a **thing**,
and when they're played, won't **break**.

Jim brought in several **bottles** and
he tapped each like a **bell**.
Most bottles sounded pretty **good**,
the rest did not **ring** well.

Julia had found a set of **cans**
and hung them from a **stick**.
She played each with a kitchen **spoon**,
which seemed to do the **trick**.

All **Alex** did was slap his **cheeks**
to play some simple tunes.
Maggie had asked her dad to **teach**
some rhythms played with **spoons**.

Kevin played on a blade of **grass**,
Sara just used a **comb**,
while **Jack** could play a **vacuum** tube
that he had brought from **home**.

Emma could **whistle**, **Mark** would **hum**,
and **Sam** just clapped his **hands**.
Jason had made an "**instrument**"
by using **rubber bands**.

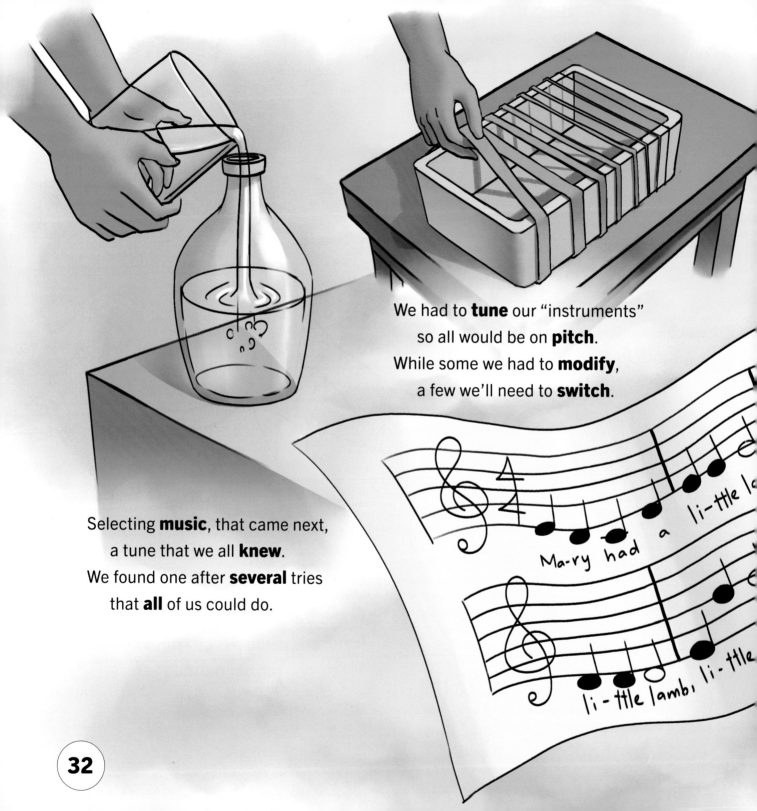

We had to **tune** our "instruments"
so all would be on **pitch**.
While some we had to **modify**,
a few we'll need to **switch**.

Selecting **music**, that came next,
a tune that we all **knew**.
We found one after **several** tries
that **all** of us could do.

Ma-ry had a li-ttle la

li - ttle lamb, li - ttle

You should have heard the **sounds** we made
but though there were some **flaws**,
still all the **kids** who **happened by**
just **laughed** with their **applause**.

We've built a fun new "**orchestra**"
and though some notes were **flat**,
we thought we did **amazingly**!
Can you IMAGINE THAT?

33

WORDS TO KNOW AND USE

After understanding each word you can try making up a sentence that uses it. The numbers at the left refer to the pages where the words appeared. Some of the words in this story have other meanings too: See page 35.

28. **"instruments"** These objects are used for playing musical notes.
    "The two instruments I enjoy most are the piano and clarinet."
    "makeshift" refers to something that has been made quickly but not well.
    "We built a makeshift dog house so our puppy will be out of the rain."
    "combined" means to put things together. "A salad combined six fruits."

29. **"orchestra"** refers to a large group playing musical instruments together.
    "An orchestra has more instruments than a jazz band."

30. **"do the trick"** refers to solving a problem or need, or doing magic.
    "Patching the tire should do the trick. It shouldn't leak anymore."
    "rhythms" refers to the beat of music. "That music has a nice rhythm."

31. **"vacuum"** is a power cleaner that sucks up dirt.
    "Mom has a new vacuum cleaner."

32 **"pitch"** is a correct sound for a musical note. "She sings with perfect pitch."
    "modify" is to change things a bit. "I can modify the heat by using a fan."
    "switch" means to change places or things. "I'll switch the TV channels."
    "several" refers to more than a few things. "I like several kinds of jam."

33. **"flaws"** refers to errors or mistakes. "I had three flaws in my report."
    "happened" refers to something that took place in the past.
    "We won our first game. It happened last week."

ACTIVITIES

Have you ever thought about playing a musical instrument that you made? What materials would you use to make it, and what kinds of sounds do you think it might make? What tunes would you play? You have seen the different instruments others have made without any of them being bought at a store. You may have thought of one that is not like any of those. You may have friends or family members who would enjoy making and playing instruments with you. It could become a musical group that performs for others. What would you name your musical group? What kind of music would you play? You could even write a story about the instrument you made, and include a drawing of it.

THINGS YOU HAVE JUST LEARNED

You have learned more words, and two of them have double meanings. **Pitch** refers to perfect tones. It is also used in baseball, when a player will **pitch** a ball to the batter. **Switch** can mean to change something and it can also mean to turn something off or on. "I will **switch** the lights off when I leave."

You have learned to read, pronounce, use, spell, and understand some words you may only have heard before. All this learning means that you are **growing mentally**. When you enjoy sharing thoughts with others, this is a part of your **social growth**. By combining what you **learn**, **do**, **think**, **share**, and **feel good about**, you are growing four ways at once: **Physically**, **socially**, **emotionally**, and **mentally**. It is possible to grow in **four** different **ways** at the same time!

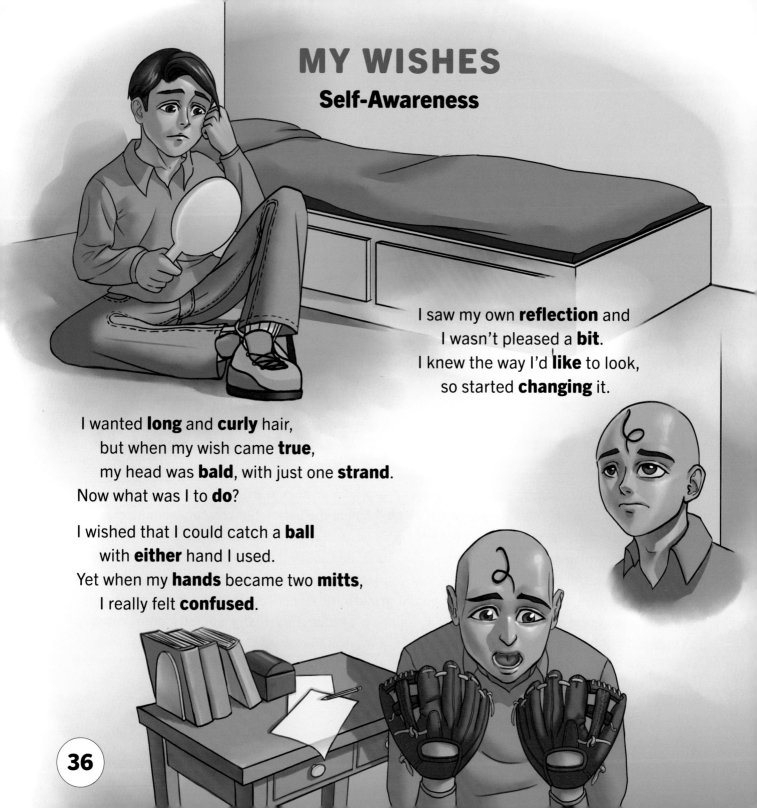

MY WISHES
Self-Awareness

I saw my own **reflection** and
I wasn't pleased a **bit**.
I knew the way I'd **like** to look,
so started **changing** it.

I wanted **long** and **curly** hair,
but when my wish came **true**,
my head was **bald**, with just one **strand**.
Now what was I to **do**?

I wished that I could catch a **ball**
with **either** hand I used.
Yet when my **hands** became two **mitts**,
I really felt **confused**.

Then next I wished to be so **strong**
that bullies won't come **near**.
But bullies said I **smelled** too bad,
and yelled, "Get **out** of here!"

That's when I wished my **family**
would just leave me **alone**.
I didn't mean I should be left
completely on my **own**.

37

I wished to have a **brighter** mind,
but much to my **surprise**,
my head lit like a brilliant **bulb**
that really **hurt** my **eyes**.

I wanted to be **taller**, but
neglected to **explain**.
So when I grew a longer **neck**,
to whom could I **complain**?

I said I'd like to have clean **nails**
that always would look **good**.
I didn't think my **wish** could be
so **poorly** understood.

And when I wished that I could **fly**,
I really meant, "a **plane**."
So when I grew two graceful **wings**,
I asked, "Will these **remain**?"

I wondered why my **every** wish
   was like a **trick** on me.
My words were twisted all **around**,
   like **jokes** made **playfully**.

Right after every wish went **wrong**
   I tried to figure **why**.
That's when I wished them all **away**,
   and made one **final** try.

My **last** wish was that I would be
  the way I'd been **before**.
I'd used up **all** my wishes then
  and didn't ask for **more**.

I'm **happy** now, I'm quite **myself**.
I'm **pleased** with what I see.
I look at my **reflection**, and
Imagine That! I'M ME!

41

WORDS TO KNOW AND USE

After understanding each word, you can try making up a sentence that uses it. The numbers at the left refer to the pages where the words appeared.

36. **"reflection"** is like seeing yourself in a mirror.
"I saw my reflection in the store window."
"strand" refers to a single hair or a few hairs that hold together.
"The wind blew a strand of hair in my eye."
"either hand" refers to using the right or the left hand.
"I can write quite well with either hand I use."
"mitts" are baseball gloves. "We use mitts for catching hard balls."
"confused" means to be mixed up or not understanding clearly.
"Your answer wasn't very clear, so I'm confused."

37. **"completely"** is another way of saying totally. "I completely forgot."

38. **"brilliant"** refers to something that is very bright, like the sun.
"The sun was so brilliant that I had to wear sunglasses."
"neglected" refers to something that was not done or cared for.
"I neglected to finish everything that I planned to do."

39. **"remain"** refers to something or someone who didn't go away.
"The stains on my shirt remain, even though it was washed twice."

40. **"twisted"** refers to something that is mixed up or bent around.
"You've twisted my words. You've mixed up what I meant."
"playfully" refers to words or actions that are said or done in fun.
"It wasn't done playfully. I splashed you by accident."
"final" refers to the last one. "I received a B+ on the final test."

ACTIVITIES

Did you ever wish for something that came true? Were you surprised when it really happened? Was it exactly what you expected, or different in some way? What was it? If you were pleased with it, could you write a story about a wish that came true, and then draw a picture that shows what it was that you wanted so much?

THINGS YOU HAVE JUST LEARNED

What kinds of things do you like to wish for? Have you ever planned to actually help a wish come true? The more you learn by watching, listening, and reading, the more you will be able to understand what things are really possible. Every time you write or tell a story, you are learning to use words that help others to understand you better. Learning to put your thoughts into words is a very useful skill. Whenever you draw, paint, build something, write, or speak, you are improving and increasing your abilities. By combining all of these you are growing **physically**, **mentally**, **socially**, and **emotionally**. Once again, you have learned that you can grow in four different ways at the same time. (See page 27.)

    If you would like to learn a HUGE word, here's a fun one. Just try saying **am-bi-dex-trous**. **Ambidextrous** is another way of saying that some people can do things with either hand: writing, throwing a ball, eating, or drawing. You now know a **12 LETTER word**. It is amazing how much you can learn and grow, just by reading and trying what's on these last **eight pages**.

THE DARE
Decision Making

Someone I know just likes to **dare**,
to see what kids will **do**.
He has them do the things he **won't**.
Believe me, this is **true**.

The dares he makes are **harmful** ones,
the kind he knows are **wrong**.
He'll watch to see what happens **next**,
though he knows all **along**.

If kids refuse he calls them **names**,
like, "You're a **scaredy**-cat."
One boy he dared said, "**No**, I **won't**!"
He feels quite **proud** of that.

The darer said, "Just climb that **fence**,
  and pick some **grapes** to eat.
The grower knows they're **good** for kids,
  and gives them as a **treat**."

I went to **see** the kid who dares.
I really was **upset**,
  because he **bullied** younger kids.
It's really **good** we met.

TRESPASSERS
WILL BE
FINED!!

I asked, "Why does that sign **warn** folks,
  '**Trespassers** will be **fined**?'
Does it say, 'Please steal my grapes,
  since I don't **really** mind?'"

He said, "That sign's for **older** folks,
  for **kids**, it's quite **okay**.
The owner tells me when they're **ripe**.
I had some **yesterday**."

"Then you don't **know**, these grapes are **grown**
  for one thing: making **wine**.
You just like getting kids in **bad**.
You're safe, so you feel **fine**!

"My **father** knows the owner and
  these grapes ripen in **June**.
For anyone who eats them **now**,
  they'd be **sick** very soon."

"Let's go and see the **owner** now
and **tell** him what you said
about the **grapes** that you've enjoyed,
after the **sign** you read.

"Now I **dare** you to **talk** with him,
then **you** can pay the fine.
But if he says, 'Just help **yourself**!'
I'll know this error's **mine**."

It's funny how his story **changed**.
He stopped his game of "**dare**."
He learned some kids are **gullible**,
and he should act with **care**.

47

Friends don't get **friends** in **trouble**, and
they don't play harmful **jokes**.
So if he wants to be our **friend**,
he won't **dare** other folks.

The **darer** hadn't thought about
the **problems** dares create,
or that he would have made kids **sick**,
from what they **picked** and **ate**.

Each dare is like a big **mistake**
that can't help **anyone**.
It only leads to **problems** when
you **could** be having **fun**.

48

For him, a dare's a "**game**" to play,
 so this was nothing **new**,
 but he had lost the **trust** of kids,
 his chance for **friendships**, too.

What really works for **everyone**:
 "**Think** first and then decide!"
Some problems **often** happen when
 precaution isn't tried.

If someone plays "I **dare** you" games,
 why not just **walk away**?
You're **far** too smart to fall for dares.
IMAGINE THAT! DON'T PLAY!

WORDS TO KNOW AND USE

After understanding each word, you can try making up a sentence that uses it. The numbers at the left refer to the pages where the words appeared. One of the words in this story has other meanings: See the lower part of page 51.

44. **"someone"** refers to a person. "Let's invite someone to go with us."
   "believe" is to know that something is true. "I believe what she said."
   "all along" refers to all the time. "I knew he was joking all along."
   "refuse" is not to do something you're told. "I refuse to do that."
   "scaredy-cat" is name calling of one who is afraid to do something.
      "You're a scaredy-cat, afraid to go outside because of thunder."

45. **"bullied"** is being pressured or threatened to do things you don't want to do.
      "He was bullied, but told the bully it would be stupid do what he said."
   "trespassers" refers to someone who enters a place against the law.
      "The trespassers went onto private land after being warned not to."
   "fined" refers to paying money for doing something that is against the law.
      "He was fined for riding his bike on the wrong side of the road."

46. **"yesterday"** refers to the day before today. "Yesterday was Friday."

47. **"gullible"** refers to someone who is easily fooled.
      "If you believe that crazy story, you must be very gullible."

48. **"mistake"** refers to an error. "I made a mistake on my spelling test."

49. **"trust"** is to believe in someone who is honest and does the right thing.
      "I know that I can always trust him, because he's always honest and fair."
   "precaution" is a safety measure you take to avoid a problem.
      "I took the precaution of locking the gate so our dog won't get out."

ACTIVITIES

Has anyone ever dared you to do something? What were you dared to do and how did it make you feel? What did you decide to do? Why do you think you were dared? How do you feel about people who dare others? Could you write a story about someone who was dared, and what they said and did about it?

THINGS YOU HAVE JUST LEARNED

You have learned how some people feel when they are dared, and what they did or said to the bully. When you realize a few of the reasons why some people bully others, this could help you to **grow socially** and **emotionally**. Being kind, considerate, and helpful are **social** skills that can add to how good you feel about yourself. The more you learn about how and why people behave as they do, the more you can understand them and yourself, too.

Some words can mean three or more things. **<u>Fine</u>** can mean that it's all right to do what you asked about, and "I feel **fine**," refers to feeling good: "I'm **fine**, thank you" is sometimes just a quick, easy way to answer a person who asks how you are. It doesn't always mean that you are really feeling good. **Fine** is also used to describe a day, or the weather: "Today is a **fine** day for swimming!"

There is so much to learn about words and how to spell, pronounce, use, and understand them. Sometimes it's important to know the person who's talking, because their tone and inflections can suggest a very different meaning.

FORGETTING AND REMINDERS

Our minds are amazing thinking and memory machines. They can help us to memorize information, recognize people, remember phone numbers and directions, how to do daily tasks, how not to make the same mistake twice, and MUCH MORE. No one likes to say, "I'm sorry. I just forgot." So it's good to be aware of the things that can make us forget. Some common ones are a sudden loud noise, an unexpected visitor, having too much to think about, being worried or very tired, being interrupted, not feeling well, and even not having a very good memory. Luckily there are some easy tricks for helping us remember, and they are used by people of all ages.

REMINDER NOTES: There are always things that don't happen often and that you don't want to forget, like "Call Aunt Jane tonight." "Jack's birthday is Saturday." "Book due Monday." Some people write little notes and tape them on the refrigerator, their lunch box, or some other place that they can't miss. Since forgetting can be easy to do, we each need to find ways that work best for us.

SCHEDULES: If you have things that don't happen often, try making a list of what has to be done during the week, or use a calendar to note what you need to remember. This saves your memory for the things that are easier to remember.

PASSING THROUGH A DOOR: If you have ever thought of something you needed, and walked through a door to get it, you may have found that suddenly you forgot what it was that you wanted to get. All you may need to do, is go back through that door to the room where you knew what to get. You may suddenly remember what you wanted. Most of us use little memory tricks as helpers.

OUR AMAZING MEMORIES

You may be surprised by the natural abilities we have for remembering. Some folks have good memories for certain things: Names, faces, scents and flavors, childhood experiences, numbers, directions, music, dances, poems, old sayings, etc. Some memory abilities are inherited and others are learned, but we all need to find our own best ways to remember. You may remember better when you write things down or read them twice. Some remember well if they take notes, tell or explain the information to someone, or use what they just learned right away. If a student owns the book that's being read, they sometimes underline the important parts so they are easy to find again. Others put a strip of paper with a reminder word at the top, and have it stick out of that page so they can read it again later.

You may know someone who is good at remembering dates, addresses, and phone numbers. Some remember names and faces, or they can go to a place they've never been, and find it again years later. Others can tell you what happened to them a long time ago, and describe it as if it happened yesterday.

If you forget to feed your puppy, it might whine, bark, stand in your way, bring the empty bowl to you, or pull on your clothes to remind you, because pets have memories too. They have their own ways of getting your attention and letting you know what you forgot to do for them. Sometimes they are just asking for help.

You can learn many new things as you read, and a good way to remember them is to use them or talk about them with someone right away. You will be learning many different and fun things to share, and sharing new information is a good way not to forget. This also encourages people to share information with you.

STAINED GLASS
Art Activity

A see-through window has **clear** glass,
some windows have **designs**.
Others have shapes of **colored** glass
with lead **dividing** lines.

They're known as **stained glass** windows and
when **sunlight's** shining through,
they often are quite **beautiful**
for **everyone** to view.

To find the **best** pane for display,
the window needs **sunshine**.
Measure the window's **height** and **width**,
then plan your **own** design.

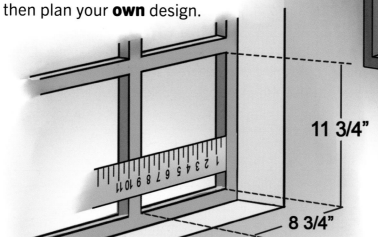

11 3/4"

8 3/4"

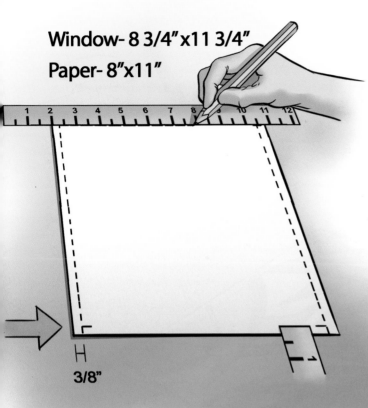

Window- 8 3/4"x11 3/4"
Paper- 8"x11"

3/8"

You'll use white paper **cut** to **size**,
and draw a **taping** line,
where tape, **NOT OIL**, will need to go
on your **finished** design.

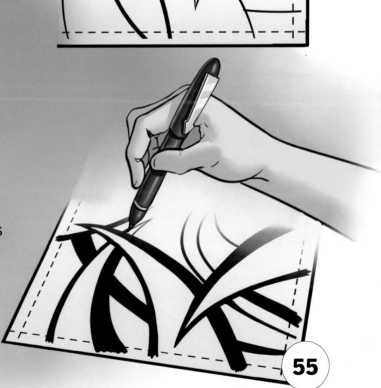

Some pencil lines must reach **tape** lines,
and when your art looks **fine**,
use **permanent black marking pen**
to blacken **every** line.

There should be ample open space.
Lines can be **thick** and **thin**,
and when you've finished all **black** lines
it's time to **color in**.

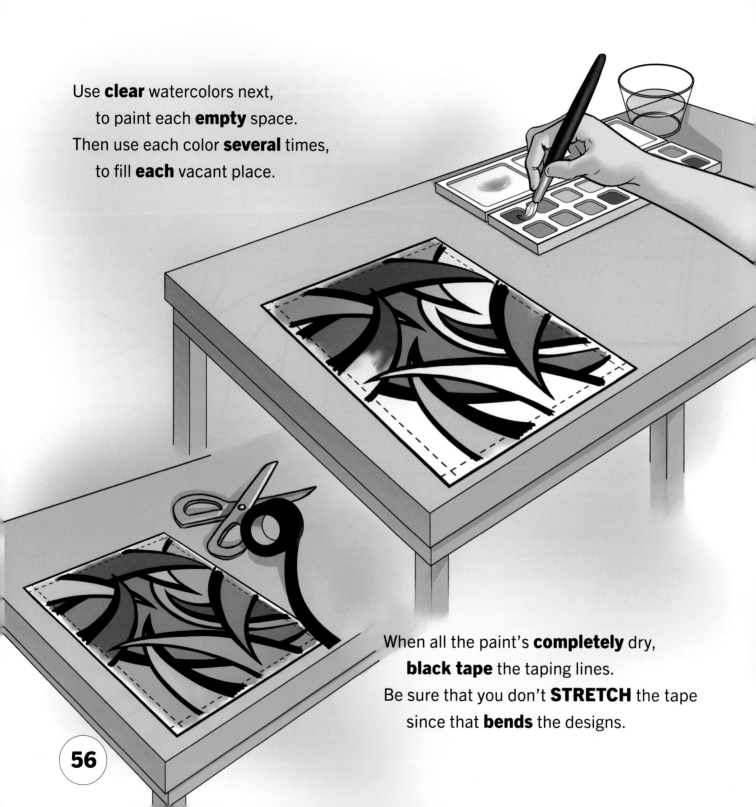

Use **clear** watercolors next,
to paint each **empty** space.
Then use each color **several** times,
to fill **each** vacant place.

When all the paint's **completely** dry,
black tape the taping lines.
Be sure that you don't **STRETCH** the tape
since that **bends** the designs.

56

Now, spread some sheets of **newspaper**.
Make sure you **smooth** them **out**.
Pour **salad** oil in a dish,
and find a **rag** about.

Next turn your painting **over** so
the tape will not get stuck!
Then **dip** the rag and **oil** the **back**,
but **NOT THE TAPE**. Good luck.

If all the colors don't **show through**,
just oil the back **again**.
When you can see **all** colors well,
wipe with a **dry** rag then.

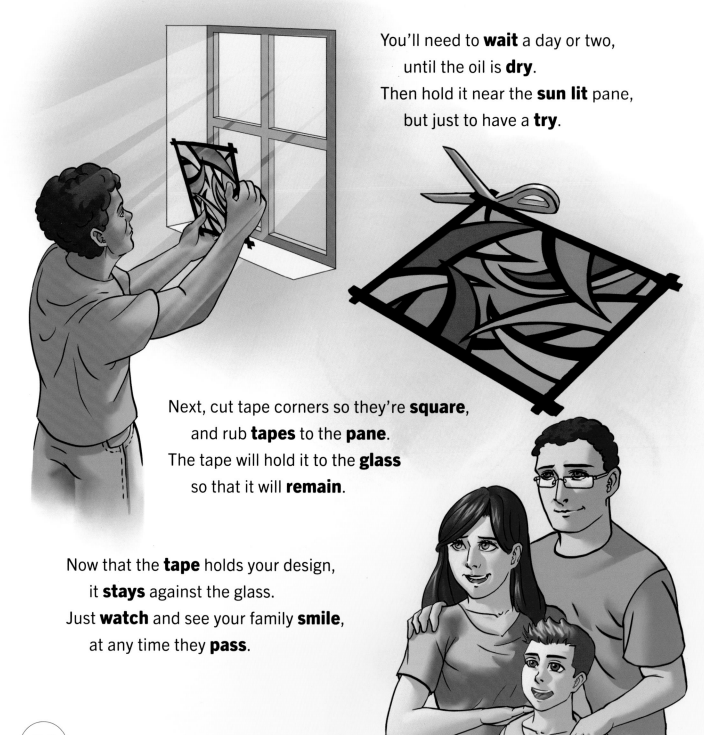

You'll need to **wait** a day or two,
until the oil is **dry**.
Then hold it near the **sun lit** pane,
but just to have a **try**.

Next, cut tape corners so they're **square**,
and rub **tapes** to the **pane**.
The tape will hold it to the **glass**
so that it will **remain**.

Now that the **tape** holds your design,
it **stays** against the glass.
Just **watch** and see your family **smile**,
at any time they **pass**.

58

Your **friends** may ask you how it's **made**,
and might try **making** one.
You could be like a **teacher** then,
if you **show** how it's done.

In time, the **sun** makes colors **fade**,
but **making** it was **fun**.
So why not use your skills **again**,
to do a **different** one.

You'll find that people **notice** them,
and try to **understand**,
who could have **made** them, and may say,
"Imagine That! ... They're GRAND!"

WORDS TO KNOW AND USE

After understanding each word, you can try making up a sentence that uses it. The numbers at the left refer to the pages where the words appeared. Some of the words in this story have other meanings too: See page 61.

54. **"lead"** is a heavy metal used to hold stained glass pieces in place.
"Did you know there is metal in pencils? They are called lead pencils."
"dividing lines" refers to lines which separate parts of the design.
"Dividing lines on courts for sports mark the 'out of bounds' area."
"display" is an arrangement to be enjoyed. "Our projects are on display."
"measure" means to use some type of ruler to learn the size of things.
"Dad used a tape measure to see how tall I am."

55. **"taping line"** means the line where a piece of tape is to be placed.
"The taping line was drawn near the edge of the artwork."
"permanent" means that it will last a very long time.
"These are my permanent teeth, not my baby teeth."

56. **"completely"** means "totally." "I was completely exhausted after my race."

57. **"smooth"** is to press or pull something to make it lay flat.
"I ironed a sheet to smooth out the wrinkles."
"show through" means to look at one side and see the other side through it.
"This jacket is so thin that the color of my shirt can show through."

58. **"remain"** is to stay in place. "My friends need to leave but I will remain."

59. **"understand"** is to know the meaning of something that is said or done.
"I have learned the rules, so I understand how the game is played."

ACTIVITIES

Except for the oiling and taping stages, these basic designs can be used for ornaments to hang up, mobiles, kites, and decorations. The outside edges don't need to be straight lines, and the shapes can even be cut out and displayed.

THINGS YOU HAVE JUST LEARNED

You have learned to repeat colors in different parts of your design. This is called balancing the colors. By making similar shapes of different sizes you have used variety in your artwork to make it more interesting.

Here are some words that have extra meanings. To **measure** can be to find the size in feet and inches, but **measure** can also refer to a person's talent. "He has shown the true **measure** of his ability." **Black** can refer to a color or darkness, but also to a person's character. "My name was **blackened** because I told a lie." **Stretch** can mean to make something longer or to be getting close to a place. "We are on the home **stretch**," which means "nearly there." Because your mind is growing from all that you are learning, you are having **mental growth**. Learning makes each day an adventure.

MY FUTURE
Planning Ahead

I wonder where I'll **be** someday.
What are the things I'll **do**,
   and who will be the **friends** I have?
I think about **that** too.

Where will I **live**, and **work**, and **play**?
Will I still ride a **bike**?
How will the world have **changed** by then,
   and what will it be **like**?

There's much I'll need to **think** about,
like all the ways I'll **change**.
This growing up is **new** to me,
and **some** of it seems **strange**.

It may be wise to look **ahead**
and plan how life might **be**.
Right now, I know that **much** of this
is **really** up to **me**.

AGE
18 Graduate
high School
19 Attend College
majoring in
industrial design
23 Graduate
24 Attend graduate
School in product
design

Sometimes I wonder where I'll **live**,
maybe the **countryside**.
Will I prefer an **ocean** view?
There's much that **I'll** decide.

Perhaps I'll drive a **mini-van**,
maybe a **hybrid** one.
My car might be a **special** type,
fueled mainly by the **sun**.

I'll meet **more** people as I grow,
 ones I've not **known** before.
There'll be some grand adventures too,
 and I'll keep having **more**.

I might like camping in the **woods**
 and even sail a **boat**.
Maybe I'll visit other **lands**
 though some might be **remote**.

Will I still like the **games** I play,
or learn **new** ones by then,
that are such fun for **everyone**
we'll want to play **again**?

I'd like to try **improving** things,
to make folks **happier**.
They ought to have a chance to **choose**
the things that **they'd** prefer.

I'll study subjects I like **most**
so when I am **employed**,
I'll really want to do my **best**
at all that I've **enjoyed**.

And **somehow** as I find my way,
I'm **certain** I will be,
a person who I'm pleased to **know**,
and I'll be **proud** of me.

It's good to think about this **now**.
There's much I'd like to **do**.
I'll **hope** to meet some **brand new** friends.
IMAGINE THAT! LIKE YOU!

WORDS TO KNOW AND USE

After understanding each word, you can try making up a sentence that uses it. The numbers at the left refer to the pages where the words appeared. Some of the words in this story have other meanings too: See page 69.

62. **"someday"** refers to a time in the future. "Someday I might visit New York."

63. **"strange"** means odd or unusual. "It seemed strange to have nothing to do."
    "ahead" refers to something in front of you. "Watch out for those cars ahead."

64. **"countryside"** refers to areas away from the city with larger, open spaces.
    "If I lived in the countryside, my family could have a horse."
    "prefer" refers to liking something better. "I really prefer vanilla ice cream."
    "decide" refers to having a choice to make, or making a decision.
    "I can't decide what I'd like to do this weekend."
    "hybrid" refers to a vehicle that runs on both gasoline and batteries.
    "Many cars are hybrid types, which help to keep the air cleaner."
    "fueled" refers to what is used to power a car, motor, heater, or stove.
    "Some cars are fueled by diesel instead of gasoline."

65. **"adventures"** refers to doing things that are exciting or unexpected.
    "Climbing along the mountain trails was quite an adventure."
    "sail" refers to going out on a lake or ocean in a boat with sails.
    "There's a light wind today, so it's a good day to sail."

66. **"everyone"** refers to all of the people. "Everyone likes my puppy."
    "employed" refers to having a paying job. "The bank employed her."

67. **"somehow"** is like saying, "for some reason," but not knowing how or why.
    "Somehow this stew tastes even better today than it did last night."

ACTIVITIES

After reading the story, did you think of things you would like to do someday? Where would you like to live or visit? What would you enjoy learning, and what kind of work might you do? How old will you be when these changes begin? Why not write about something you would enjoy doing someday and illustrate it. Then you could think about, imagine, and plan the future that you would like.

THINGS YOU HAVE JUST LEARNED

You have learned about someone else's thoughts for the future. Did they give you ideas about your own future? Did you know that your future actually starts a minute from now? Try thinking about what you might be doing ten days or ten years from now. There are so many possibilities when you plan ahead.

Whenever you plan for or think about something new, you are using your mind. This includes reading and learning new words and having new ideas. Doing this helps you **grow mentally**. If you discuss your hopes and dreams, and share thoughts with others, you could **grow socially** too.

Some of the words you learned have two meanings. **View** can refer to something you see, but also something you think or believe. "What's your **view** about what happened today?" If a person says, "You are **sailing** through your chores today," it means you are working quickly, not that you are **sailing** a boat.

Creative Eyes
Creative and Imaginative Thinking

Today, I saw so **many** things
    I'd never **seen** before.
So I just took some time to **look**
    and see if there were **more**.

I found a giant **water** snake,
    as long as 20 **feet.**
I left it sleeping in the **pond,**
    while I made my **retreat.**

Then next I saw a bearded **man**
who stared right **back** at me.
I only saw his weathered **face**
since he hid in a **tree**.

I turned and nearly **stepped** on it,
a **reptile** on the ground.
It didn't try to run **away**
or even make a **sound**.

71

That's when I looked up to the **sky,**
 and saw to my **surprise,**
 a giant **dragon** in the clouds.
I can't believe my **eyes**!

Why would these things **appear** to me,
 sights no one **else** has seen?
I found them almost **frightening**
 and wondered what they **mean**.

That's when I saw a **friend** of mine.
Perhaps **he'd** seen them, **too**.
He might take time to **tell** me if
   these things I've seen are **true**.

He said, "You can **forget** it since
   such things could not be **real**.
To ease your mind, let's have a **look**
   and see what we **reveal**."

He took my **hand** so I'd feel **safe**.
We walked to where I'd **been**.
I showed him **each** and **every** one,
... but all he did was **grin**.

"Your eyes are quite **remarkable**.
You've helped **me** see them, **too**.
Those sights I thought could **never** be,
... are **ABSOLUTELY TRUE**!"

"That water snake's a **garden** hose,
this tree trunk's like a **man**.
Your **reptile**'s simply mud and twigs.
Things **I** can't see, **YOU CAN**!

"Your **dragon** cloud has long since moved,
and what had **frightened** you,
has now been changed by **wind** and **sun**
to just a **lovely** view.

"I've always seen the basic **facts**
of what I'm **looking** at.
But through your young, **creative** eyes,
I SEE! IMAGINE THAT!"

WORDS TO KNOW AND USE

After understanding each word, you can try making up a sentence that uses it. The numbers at the left refer to the pages where the words appeared. One of the words in this story has another meaning too: See page 77.

70. **"retreat"** means to back up to where you are safe from harm.
    "We made a wise retreat, so no one was injured during the storm."

71. **"bearded man"** means a man who doesn't shave the hair on his face.
    "A bearded man walked into the barber shop for a haircut."
    "weathered face" is having rough, leathery skin from often being in severe weather.
    "By often staying outside in icy winds or very hot sun, he has a weathered face."
    "reptile" refers to an animal with scales that crawls on its stomach.
    "A snake is a reptile, and so is a lizard."

72. **"surprise"** is to have something unexpected happen. "It's a surprise party!"
    "dragon" is a big, imaginary monster that has wings and breathes fire.
    "I wonder if there is a friendly dragon that is helpful to people?"
    "frightening" refers to being afraid. "That loud noise was frightening."

73. **"perhaps"** is another way of saying "maybe." "Perhaps I'll go tomorrow."
    "ease your mind" refers to not being worried or concerned.
    "You can ease your mind. There is no need to worry. It's really safe."
    "reveal" means that something unexpected is seen or heard.
    "Do you want me to reveal the surprise ending of the story?"

74. **"remarkable"** means very unusual. "What you've made is quite remarkable!"
    "absolutely" refers to something you are sure of. "It's absolutely true."

75. **"trunk"** refers to the main body of a tree. "That tree trunk is HUGE!"

ACTIVITIES

Did you ever see something for a moment and think it was something else? What were you looking at, and what did it look like? Did anyone else see it too? Why not write a story about it and draw a picture of what it really was and what you thought it was?

THINGS YOU HAVE JUST LEARNED

Having an imagination is fun because it gives you ideas that are original. It's a bit like having your own private wonderland of thoughts. At times, what you see can make you smile and want to tell someone about it. Developing creativity and imagination are a part of your **mental growth**. People who are creative and have original ideas sometimes become artists, musicians, authors, dancers, composers, fabric or clothing designers, architects, designers, inventors, or have other special talents which can be trained. They often lose track of time because they are enjoying their work so much. They are seldom bored because there are always things that interest them. They might look at something and think, "I could make that better, easier to use, more fun, safer, or less expensive." Solving problems is fun for them.

The word **trunk** can refer to the main body of a tree, an elephant's **trunk**, the torso or body of a person, or even the back part of a car where things can be carried. "Mom puts groceries in the **trunk** of our car." Some words can sound alike, but have different spellings and meanings: "The **two** of us are going **to** the store, **too**." Words and spelling can be full of interesting surprises.

IMAGINATION AND CREATIVITY

These two amazing words are the reason why we have bicycles and roller skates, wheel barrows, cars, and HUNDREDS of other things that roll and carry things and people. A prehistoric person might have picked up a thin round stone and held the center between his thumb and finger and rolled it on his hand or on the ground. Another ancient human might have watched him and thought of putting a hole in the middle of the flat, circular stone, and poking a small stick in the hole. That way he could hold the stick and roll the stone.

Years later, another early human might have watched someone rolling their flat stones, and thought it would be better to have a second stone at the other end of the stick. These ideas may have increased over hundreds of years, until an imaginative person decided to make two much larger round, flat shapes with a longer stick running to the centers of the two round shapes and thought, "This isn't just a toy."

Centuries later, someone may have thought of using a longer stick to attach to the center of the stick holding the circular stones. That way, it could be pulled and rolled behind. Maybe a child climbed on the pulling stick and laughed as she was rolled along. No one really knows how it all began, but if it were not for some ancient humans being curious, trying their ideas, other people imagining the possibilities, and still others creating things that rolled, our world would be very different. How different would your own life be without wheels? Be grateful for curiosity, experimenting, imagining, and creating that made wheels have many uses. Even a yo-yo is just two wheels joined with a tiny stick, and rolled up and down on a piece of string.

THE WONDER OF WORDS

If it weren't for words, we would probably still be grunting at each other, making faces, pointing at things, scratching a few marks on the ground, or acting out our needs and feelings. Gradually, in the language of early people, grunts became sounds, and the sounds were changed by the way they happened to use their tongues, shaped their lips, and let air out of their mouths. The sounds became more and more varied, and each one began to have a separate meaning. No one knows how many centuries it took for those marks and symbols on the ground that were used to mean numbers and words, to become an alphabet for a language.

You would think that after all these thousands of years we would have enough words to say everything that needed to be said. But people are imaginative, and keep thinking of new ways to say things, inventing names for new products, and making more words to describe the parts and uses. People enjoy giving different meanings to words that sound alike but are spelled differently, like the words for, four, and fore. As a result, our dictionaries keep getting thicker with each new edition. A word can even have a different meaning in another part of the country, or the same word can be said using a different accent. Other countries have different kinds of language, such as one African language that is spoken with clicking sounds. Nigeria, another African country, has over 250 different languages. One of them, Yoruba, must be spoken by using three different tones — high, medium, and low — and these tones are used in just one word. People are inventive and imaginative, and create new words, expressions, and ways of saying things in speech, chants, song, and even code. These are only a few of the Wonder of Words.

The Boxes
Construction Activity

My dad saves **lots** of boxes and
he stores them all **away**.
If I should ask to **use** a few,
I wonder what he'd **say**.

He's kept all **sorts** and **sizes** too,
this **larger** box holds **ten**.
He doesn't use them **often,** but
he **needs** one now and then.

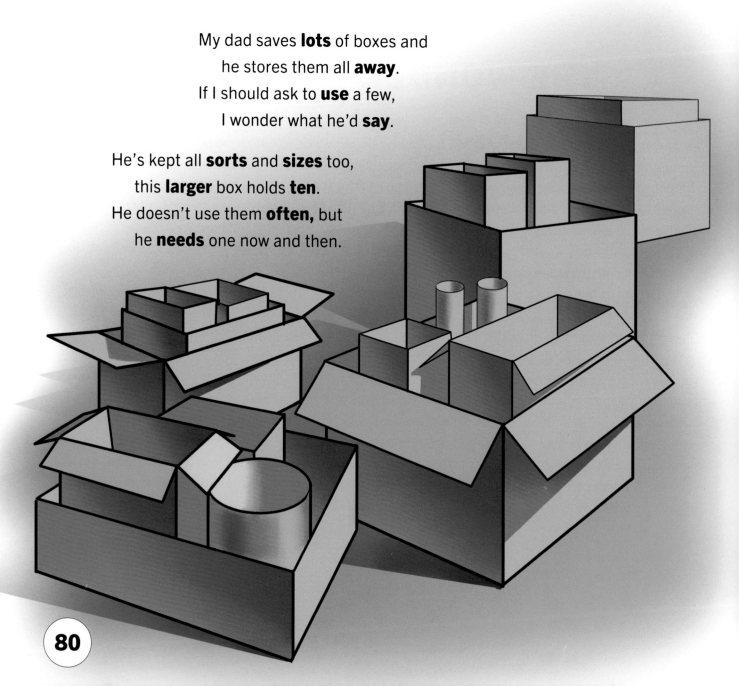

He asked me what I planned to **make**,
and when I had **explained**,
he said that I could help **myself**
so long as some **remained**.

That's when I asked to use a **knife**,
a sharp but "**safety**" one.
He chose the **perfect** tool for me.
I'll put it back when **done**.

81

This type of knife is **handy** since
the blade slides **out** and then,
when I have finished **using** it,
the blade slides **in** again.

Some **extra** blades are stored inside,
in case I need a **spare**,
and when the blade's too dull to **cut**
I'll have some **new** ones there.

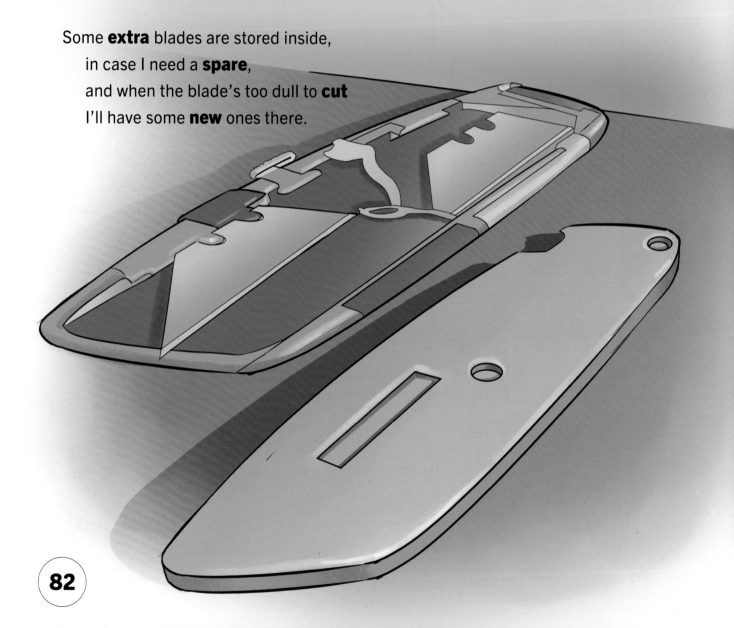

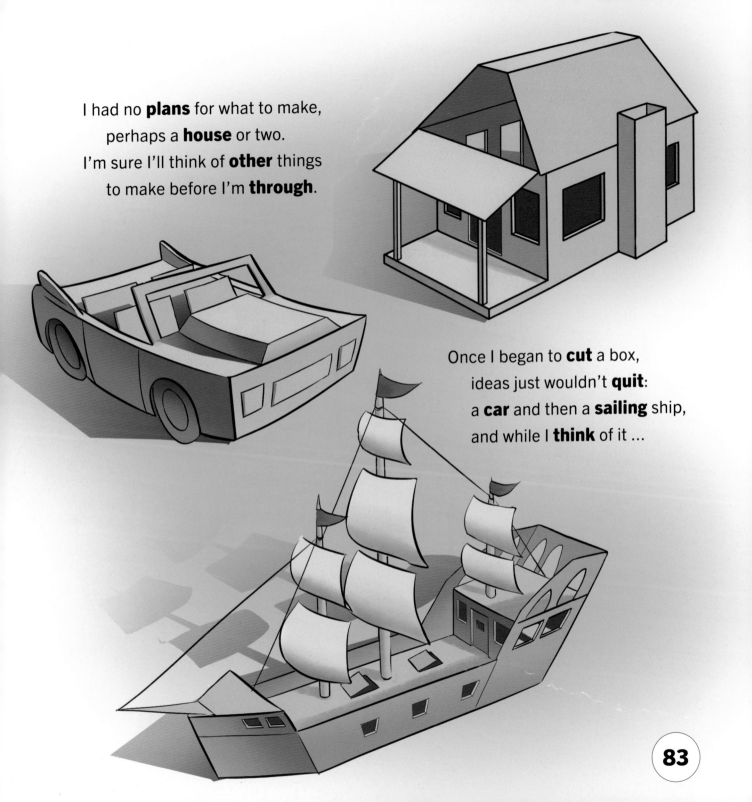

I had no **plans** for what to make,
perhaps a **house** or two.
I'm sure I'll think of **other** things
to make before I'm **through**.

Once I began to **cut** a box,
ideas just wouldn't **quit**:
a **car** and then a **sailing** ship,
and while I **think** of it ...

83

... why not a **train**, a **station** too,
some **other** things, and then,
if I don't **like** the things I've made,
I'll simply try **again**.

These boxes were just **sitting** there
while Dad collected **more**,
but now they're my **creations** that
no one has **made** before.

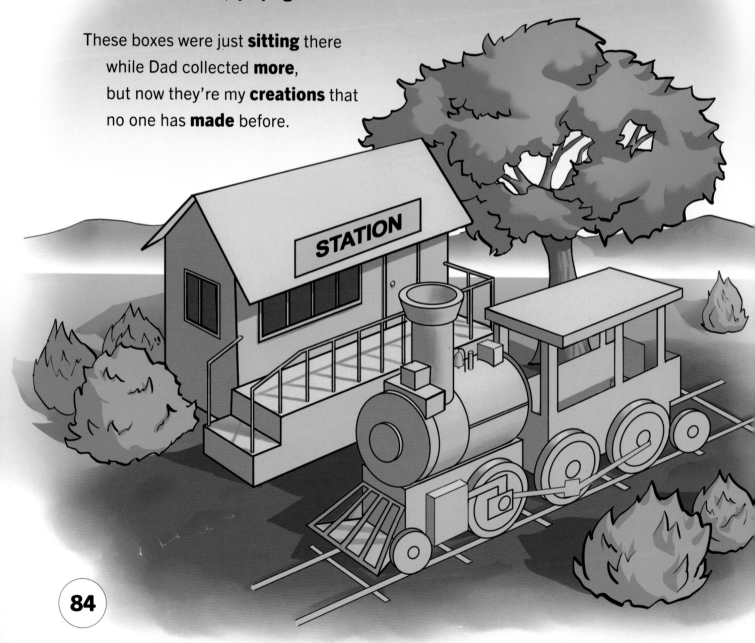

STATION

I've cut some **angled** pieces and
   I **glued** and joined each **one**.
What they'll become, it's hard to **say**,
   I'll know that when I'm **done**.

Just **look**! I've made a **masterpiece**,
   this **abstract** stands **apart**.
It's **painted** so I'm **finished** now.
Imagine That! IT'S <u>ART!</u>

85

WORDS TO KNOW AND USE

After understanding each word, you can try making a sentence that uses it. The numbers at the left refer to the pages where the words appeared. Some of the words in this story have other meanings too: See page 87.

80. **"stores"** refers to putting things away so they can be used later.
"Mother stores my socks in the second drawer of my dresser."
"wonder" refers to thinking about choices, reasons, and possibilities.
"I wonder what I should do next?"
"sorts" refers to grouping or arranging things that are similar.
"Before doing the laundry, Mom sorts out the colored clothes."

81. **"explained"** is to tell what was meant so that it is understood.
"He explained the rules of the game so that I understood them."

82 **"spare"** refers to an extra one. "It's cold tonight, I'll need a spare blanket."

83. **"through"** refers to being finished. "I'm through with all my chores."
"quit" is to stop doing something. "If something is fun, it's hard to quit."

84. **"collected"** refers to saving things to keep. "I collected sea shells."
"creations" refers to original things that people make.
"My stories and artworks are my own creations."

85. **"masterpiece"** refers to an artist's most outstanding piece of work.
"At the art gallery we saw a masterpiece that was painted by Picasso."
"abstract" refers to a thought or design that is not like real things appear.
"I drew an abstract of a face, with unusual features put at odd angles."
"stands apart" means it is noticed before any others. "That player stands apart."

ACTIVITIES

Many empty boxes are saved in cupboards, closets, and other places. Just think of all the things you could make with them by using your own ideas and your imagination. This story showed what one person made, but yours will be your own ideas, and they will be different. You could even use a box to make a game and write the rules for playing it. Thinner cardboard, like a cereal box, can even be cut with scissors and pieces can be joined with tape or glue.

THINGS YOU HAVE JUST LEARNED

All of your planning, deciding and imagining are part of your **mental growth**. If you are making something with the help of a friend, how well you work together is part of your **social growth**. The hand skills you develop as you work are part of your **physical growth**. Just one story and its activities can help you to grow in three different ways.

Here again, there are words with two meanings. **Stores** also refers to grocery **stores**, clothing **stores**, and many other types of **stores**. The word **sorts** can mean a variety of objects or activities. "All **sorts** of things went wrong, but we still won."

Once more, spelling can seem odd. In the following examples, the correct spelling is underlined. It's important to know spelling because words are not always spelled the way they sound. **Remain** sounds as if it should to be spelled **remane**, **quit** sounds like **kwit**, **station** sounds like **stayshun**, and **scissors** like **sizzers**. Some words have silent letters, like the three underlined in **through**. It's pronounced **thru**! Spelling is full of surprises!

Hidden "Treasure"

Decision Making

When I am walking by **myself**
    I always scan the **ground**.
If I would only look **ahead**
    I'd miss what might be **found**.

Each time I cross a vacant **lot**
    I take the well-used **trail**.
That's when I search for what's been **lost**,
    and very seldom **fail**.

One time I found a **pocket** knife,
  but it had rusted **tight**.
That's when a **friend** of mine remarked,
  "To **me** it looks all right."

Sometimes my **Mom** will walk with me.
She says to look **ahead**,
  "Be careful. You could **trip** and **fall**."
But I look **down** instead.

She thinks that all I'll find is **trash**,
  like old **discarded** things.
Still I prefer to search the **ground**
  to see what my **luck** brings.

89

As I was looking **down** one day,
    I saw a **kitten** there.
It tried to hide among the **weeds**,
    and had a frightened **stare**.

My voice was **soft** as I leaned down.
I heard it **hiss** a bit.
The kitten crouched, then backed **away**
    as I began to **sit**.

"**Wait**! I won't **hurt** you little one,
    I'd like to **help** somehow."
Then as I watched, it raised its **paw**
    and gave a soft "**meow**."

I thought it might be someone's **pet**
   that simply lost its **way**.
Its home could be someplace **nearby**.
It may not be a **stray**.

The kitten looked so **frightened** that
   I reached out **carefully**.
I stroked its **head**, and then I said,
   "Why not come **home** with me?"

Once tucked inside my **jacket** front,
   supported by my **arm**,
   it quickly seemed to settle **down**
   when it felt safe from **harm**.

That day I found the **owner**, and
he said, "It needs a **home**.
Each day our dog keeps **chasing** it.
That's why it wants to **roam**."

I'd learned what **caused** the kitten's fear,
and why it **hid** that way.
Their family dog had **frightened** it,
so it's **afraid** to stay.

When we reached home I told my **Mom**,
  "This kitten ran **away**.
My **searching** days are over, since
  I found 'my **prize**' today."

This big adventure **tired** it,
  the kitty's feeling **spent**.
But now well fed it's quite **secure**,
  catnapping and **content**.

My Mom declared, "You've found a **friend**,
  it's now **your** little cat.
You could call your hider, '**Treasure**.'"
I WILL! IMAGINE THAT!

WORDS TO KNOW AND USE

After understanding each word, you can try making up a sentence that uses it. The numbers at the left refer to the pages where the words appeared. Some of the words in this story have other meanings too: See page 95.

88. **"scan"** means to look for something. "I'll scan the room to find where it is."
    "seldom" means not often. "I seldom have a chance to visit my uncle."

89. **"remarked"** refers to saying something. "He remarked about my dad's new job."
    "prefer" means to want something different. "I would prefer having a dog."

90. **"frightened stare"** means someone's eyes are glaring and looking afraid.
    "During the horror movie, Mary had a frightened stare."
    "crouched" refers to stooping low. "She crouched and hid behind the sofa."
    "somehow" is another way of saying, "In some way."
    "Somehow I didn't get hurt when I fell."
    "raised" refers to lifting something. "I raised the lid of the box."

91. **"nearby"** refers to something that is close. "That store is nearby."

92. **"roam"** means to wander. "I like to roam around and find new things."
    "caused" refers to making something happen. "What caused the accident?"

93. **"reached home"** refers to arriving home. "I reached home early."
    "spent" refers to being very tired. "I felt spent after running home."
    "secure" means feeling safe. "Seat belts help me to feel secure."
    "catnapping" refers to having a short sleep. "I was just catnapping."

ACTIVITIES

Have you ever found something that you weren't looking for? Had someone lost what you found? If so, were you able to return it? What have you found that surprised you? How old were you at that time? Could you write a story about it and include a drawing of what you found?

THINGS YOU HAVE JUST LEARNED

You have learned that you need to be calm and patient when you find a frightened kitten or puppy. You may need to sit a few feet away without moving around, so that it might feel it can trust you. If you talk to it, speak softly.

Here are some things to think about when finding a stray pet. Why was it important for the boy to find the owner of the kitten? Was it good to learn why the kitten was so frightened? Is it wise to find out if a kitten might be afraid of ALL dogs? Would he take the kitten home if his dog chased cats? Should he have asked his mother if it would be alright to keep it?

You have learned to understand and use words that were new to you. Here are three more words with two meanings. **<u>Reach</u>** can mean to stretch to get something you want. It also means to arrive. "I'll **reach** home late." **<u>Vacant</u>** can mean empty, or a blank look. "She was daydreaming and had a **vacant** stare." **<u>Raised</u>** refers to where you grew up. "I was **raised** on a farm."

Some words have unexpected spellings. In these examples, the correct spelling is underlined. Maybe you think **<u>search</u>** should be spelled **surch**, the way church is spelled, and **<u>reach</u>** sounds as if it should be spelled **reech.** Learning to spell is part of **mental growth,** and having a good memory can be a big help.

Happy Endings
Self-Awareness

While playing tag, I tore my **shirt**,
  and though it's not like **new**,
  I sewed it up, and have a **look**.
I think it's **fine**, don't **you**?

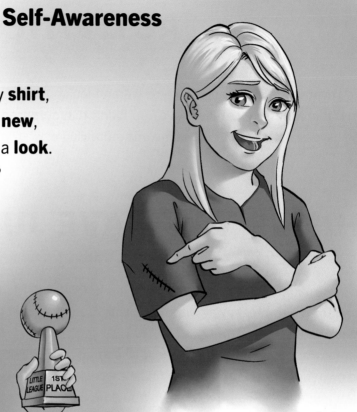

I had to slide to reach home **plate**
  and messed up all my **clothes**.
But now they are my **lucky** ones.
I won the **game** in those!

Sam rode his brand new **bike** today,
the tire had a **flat**.
I patched it and it now **holds air**.
I'm very **proud** of that.

Jane slipped and broke a **fingernail**,
that's why her nails don't **match**.
What luck, she didn't break a **bone**,
or even get a **scratch**.

The **grocery** bag a woman held,
  had spilled things on the **floor**.
When I declined her **pay** for **help**,
  she said, "You're worth much **more**!"

I lost my money for the **bus**,
  so I jogged **home** today.
I joined some **other** folks who jog,
  and had more **fun** that way.

I burned the slice of **toast** I'd made,
    but I didn't **waste** it.
Some charred food can be **good** for folks,
    so I had to **taste** it.

In our school play, I **goofed** my **lines**,
    and people **laughed** and **cheered**.
It seemed to make them **happy**, so
    I'm glad that I **appeared**.

99

When I fell down, I cut my **lip**,
while I was chasing **Ruth**.
She's sorry, but I'm **grateful** that
I didn't chip a **tooth**.

One day each month, I wash the **car**.
Our neighbor said, "You're **good**!
I'll fix your bike if you'll wash **mine**."
So I told him I **would**.

I used to have a **paper** route.
Folks paid me right **away**,
but one man **over**paid, and said,
"That's for a rainy **day**."

If I'm **upset** by what occurs
I know **right** off the **bat**,
that something **good** could happen next.
It's true. IMAGINE THAT!

WORDS TO KNOW AND USE

After understanding each word, you can try making up a sentence that uses it. The numbers at the left refer to the pages where the words appeared. Some of these words may have other meanings too: See page 103.

96. **"tore"** refers to a tear in cloth or paper. "My puppy accidentally tore my shirt."
"home plate" refers to the ending place of a home run in baseball.
　　"He reached home plate and everyone yelled 'SAFE!'"

97. **"flat"** refers to a tire that lost its air. "His front tire had a flat."
"slipped" means to slide or to fall. "She slipped on the ice and fell."
"match" means that they are alike. "My socks match."

98. **"declined"** means to refuse something. "He declined the invitation."
"jogged" refers to slow and steady running. "I jogged to the store."

99. **"waste"** refers to things that aren't saved because they are broken or spoiled.
　　"I saved what I couldn't eat. I didn't want to waste it."
"taste" means to try a little bit to see if you like it. "May I taste it?"
"goofed" refers to making a mistake. "I goofed. I forgot my books."
"appeared" refers to being seen. "She appeared from around the corner."

100. **"neighbor"** refers to someone who lives close by. "She's my neighbor."

101. **"paper route"** means the streets used when delivering newspapers.
　　"I go right past the school when I'm on my paper route."
"overpaid" means being paid too much money. "You overpaid by ten cents."
"a rainy day" refers to a time when something you've saved is needed.
　　"I'll save it for a rainy day."
"off the bat" is slang meaning "right away." "He answered right off the bat."

ACTIVITIES

Have you ever had something happen that made you feel bad, and then had something nice happen right afterward or because of it? Could you write about it and explain the problem and the good thing that occurred after that? How did you feel about the two things that you experienced? You might even make a drawing that shows more about what happened.

THINGS YOU HAVE JUST LEARNED

If something doesn't turn out the way you had hoped, you may be able to find something good that you learned from it. Maybe it could have been worse! "**Positive thinking**" is thinking of what was good or lucky about your experiences, instead of what was bad or unlucky. Those who use "positive thinking" can find that they are not upset as often when something goes wrong.

Tore can mean to run home fast. "I **tore** right home so I could tell my good news." **Slipped** can mean to do something that no one noticed. "I **slipped** quietly into the room."

Match can refer to a sporting game. "I watched the soccer **match** after school today." **Taste** can refer to making good choices. "She has excellent **taste** in gifts she buys."

Most sentences tell **WHO**, **WHAT**, **WHERE**, **WHEN**, **HOW**, and **WHY**. "In the morning (when), I (who) bike (how) to school (where). I arrive sooner (when) by biking instead of riding the bus (what), because the bus stops for kids." (why)

ARE YOU SURPRISED BY ALL YOU HAVE LEARNED?

1. Were you aware of the genes and heredity you have that came from your parents and their ancestors? You can read this again on **page 26**.

2. In the past, did you think that growing was only about getting taller or stronger, and growing new teeth and longer hair? Three other ways you grow are on **page 27**.

3. Have you thought about making your own Earth Sculptures or Stained Glass before reading about them? Now that you know how, you could show your friends how to do both. Just read the stories on **page 10** and **page 54**.

4. Before reading about it, had you thought about using your own Creativity and Imagination? You can see examples of these on **page 2** and **page 70**. You can also learn more about imagination and creativity on **page 78**.

5. Had you ever had wishes you made come true, but in a strange or unexpected way? Some wishes that had strange results start on **page 36**.

6. Have you ever thought about your plans for the future and saving money for things you would like to do or have later on? Look at **page 18** and **page 62**.

7. Constructing things can be fun to do by yourself, or with friends and family. You may want to have another look at things someone else tried. See **pages 28** and **80**, and think of things you could make using your own ideas.

8. Making your own decisions is the fun part of how you think and reason every day. When you make decisions, you are **growing mentally** because of the careful thinking and planning you do. You read about making decisions in the stories on **pages 44** and **88**.

9. Have you ever thought about writing stories, poems, or about experiences that you've had? This can be a special adventure for you. See **page vi**.

10. Do you remember all the grand new words you've learned? Have you tried making sentences using those words? If you have forgotten how many new words you've learned, just look on these pages and be AMAZED. Look on pages **8**, **16**, **24**, **34**, **42**, **50**, **60**, **68**, **76**, **86**, **94**, and **102**.

THE NEXT BOOK IN THIS SERIES

The second book of **READING IS FUN! IMAGINE THAT!** will offer other story-poems on the same six topics, with two stories on each topic.

ART ACTIVITIES:

The Kite: A child learns how to design, make, and fly a kite.

Making Ornaments: Designs are cut, shaped, and made into many things.

CONSTRUCTION ACTIVITIES:

The Door-to-Door Store: Youngsters make a cart and items to sell from it.

Coat of Arms: Friends study old designs then make their own coat of arms.

CREATIVE & IMAGINATIVE THINKING:

Driftwood Zoo: Campers walk on the beach and discover driftwood images.

The Curiosity Adventure: Questioning is one valuable way to discover things.

DECISION MAKING:

This Way or That: Children learn to consider their choices before deciding.

Choosing My Own Present: Making quick decisions vs. careful, wiser ones.

PLANNING AHEAD:

Differences: To plan ahead, there are many possibilities to consider.

What Happened and Why: Worrying can't solve problems, but thinking can.

SELF-AWARENESS:

Becoming Myself: A girl learns about herself and the qualities to enrich her life.

My Dream: A boy wants to do something of value, and he succeeds.

In this second book of the series, there is more information on the four areas of human growth. You will learn about the importance of asking questions and the value of being encouraged. There are opportunities to explore and enjoy your own ideas. Each of the story-poems could help you to use your creative and imaginative thinking. They also offer new chances for developing and expanding your abilities. At the same time **YOU CAN HAVE THE FUN OF DISCOVERING**!

ENDORSEMENTS

For the purpose of market testing, stories-poems titled "***READING IS FUN! IMAGINE THAT!***" were initially introduced as small individual booklets. They were intended to be an enriching adventure in the fun of reading and being creative. Their topics encouraged creativity and opportunities to expand personal interests and abilities. Sets of booklets were mailed to educators and professionals in this country and abroad. Their enthusiastic responses made it essential that the booklets be combined in book form that would provide more stories and also be in a more durable publication. The ages of those who read the booklets ranged from five-year-old kindergarten readers and non-readers, to an 89-year-old educator and author. The following responses were received.

Andie Cunningham, an instructor at Lewis & Clark College in Portland, Oregon, also taught kindergarten children on Fridays. She wrote, "The detail and care you've put in these stories is remarkable. I celebrated the wonderful wisdom those students reflected to me while reading your booklets."

Mosun Johnston Smith, of Nigeria, is a former teacher, principal, member of the Ministry of Education, and author of numerous books. In 1990, she was a guest of the New York State Department of Education, speaking on cultures and traditions in Africa. After reading the booklets, she wrote, "These booklets are absolutely incredible. An excellent job of inspiring children's creativity activities."

Claudine DeFaye, a former professor of Shakespearian studies at the University of Poitier, France, used the story booklets while teaching women English as a foreign language. One of her students wrote that she found the booklets "practical, playful, serious, affectionate, enigmatic, and varied."

In Japan, YiLing Chen also taught women English as a foreign language. She wrote, "They are fun to read. Both the writings and drawings are original. They are amazing. There are so many things that could be learned. One student commented she was also learning about American culture."

Booklets were sent to Ludmila Levine, Chairman of the American English Department at the Linguistics University in Nizhny Novgorod in Russia. She used them with student teachers. Several students wrote notes. "I think these booklets are perfect for children. They are colorful, bright, and the illustrations are awesome. I regret there were no such booklets in my childhood."

Tom Soma, Director of Ronald McDonald House Charities in Portland, Oregon, wrote, "Yours is a comforting voice during a challenging time. Your stories are charming. Each one is uniquely warm and inspiring, and the messages are uplifting for children and parents alike. The booklets *deserve* to be in homes across the country — and the world. They remind me of one of my all-time heroes: Mr. Rogers! They are kind, nurturing, and so encouraging."

Rosaline Turnbull, Past President of the California Parent Teacher's Association, stated that she would like to see them in all of California's elementary schools.

ABOUT THE ILLUSTRATOR

 **Isaak Lien** was born in 1984 in Hamburg, Germany, but spent his childhood and most of his life in California. Having been blessed with an enthusiastic heart for drawing since childhood, he has developed a special sensibility for art creation. Isaak's passion for the arts led him to study and graduate from the prestigious Pasadena Art Center College of Design as an illustration major and Entertainment Design minor. Currently a senior artist, Isaak has worked for the past eight years on a plethora of art projects such as children's book illustration, mural painting, card game illustrations, mobile game concept design, and production art, which includes character, map vehicle, accessories, design and digital painting. Additionally, he has taught various forms of art including sketching, painting, digital art, and anime drawing to students of various age groups. His digital paintings have been accepted into Expose 7, a book containing the finest international collections of Digital Art.

ABOUT THE AUTHOR

Ruth Radmore was born, raised, and educated in California. She wrote her first poem when she was eight, and her first story was published two years later. Those creative interests expanded from that time on. Ruth received her BA and teaching credential at UCLA, and her MA at the College of the Pacific in Central California.

While teaching, Ruth met and married another teacher, David Radmore. The couple spent their 14-month honeymoon bicycle camping in Europe, and wintered in Tangier. Later, they volunteered for the Peace Corps for two years, and taught at the Women's Training College in Nigeria. During holidays, Ruth worked at a toy factory designing and making toys and furniture, while David trained track and field athletes for the upcoming Olympic Games.

The Radmores have hosted many exchange students and friends from their travel abroad. Before retiring from teaching, Ruth began an advertising and design business and later studied Commercial Design one summer at the Art Center College of Design. Since retiring from business, she has created ceramic portraits and sculptures, and is currently writing educational children's books.

Mr. and Mrs. Radmore live on two acres in Central California, where their home has become a "fun house" for their many interests. They've enjoyed having a donkey, horses, ostriches, llamas, and special in-home pets. Both believe "There should be joy in each day," and that "If dreams have meaning and value, they should be realized." Their new dreams continue.

About SparkPress

SparkPress is an independent, hybrid imprint focused on merging the best of the traditional publishing model with new and innovative strategies. We deliver high-quality, entertaining, and engaging content that enhances readers' lives. We are proud to bring to market a list of *New York Times* best-selling, award-winning, and debut authors who represent a wide array of genres, as well as our established, industry-wide reputation for creative, results-driven success in working with authors. SparkPress, a BookSparks imprint, is a division of SparkPoint Studio LLC.

Learn more at GoSparkPress.com